WEIMAR AND NAZI GERMANY, 1918-1939

An Edexcel Study Guide; Modern Depth Study

LOUGHLIN SWEENEY

First published in 2021 by Accolade Tuition Ltd
71-75 Shelton Street
Covent Garden
London WC2H 9JQ
www.accoladetuition.com
info@accoladetuition.com

Copyright © 2021 by Loughlin Sweeney

The right of Loughlin Sweeney to be identified as the author of this work has been asserted by him in accordance with the Copyright, Designs and Patents Act 1988.

All rights reserved. No part of this book may be reproduced in any form or by any electronic or mechanical means, including information storage and retrieval systems, without written permission from the author, except for the use of brief quotations in a book review.

ISBN 978-1-913988-20-3

FIRST EDITION
1 3 5 7 9 10 8 6 4 2

Image on Page v (top left) & Page vi: Designed by stories / Freepik

Image, Page 3. ('Berlin, Reichspräsidentenwahl, Wahlwerbung') Copyright © Bundesarchiv, Bild 102-13203A. Licensed under CC-BY-SA 3.0:https://creativecommons.org/licenses/by-sa/3.0/de/legalcode.
Source: https://commons.wikimedia.org/wiki/File:Bundesarchiv_Bild_102-13203A,_Berlin,_Reichspräsidentenwahl,_Wahlwerbung.jpg

Image, Page 13. ('KAS-Politischer Gegner, Nationalsozialisten-Bild-15738-2') Copyright © Theo Matejko. Permission for use: Archiv für Christlich-Demokratische Politik (ACDP). Licensed under CC-BY-SA 3.0.
Source: https://commons.wikimedia.org/wiki/File:KAS-Politischer_Gegner,_Nationalsozialisten-Bild-15738-2.jpg

Image, Page 59. ('Kapp-Putsch, Berlin') Copyright © Bundesarchiv, Bild 146-1970-051-65 / Haeckel, Otto. Licensed under CC-BY-SA 3.0.
Source: https://commons.wikimedia.org/wiki/File:Bundesarchiv_Bild_146-1970-051-65,_Kapp-Putsch,_Berlin.jpg

---

Secondary Sources

Evans, Richard J, *The Third Reich in Power* (London: Penguin, 2006).

Henig, Ruth, *The Weimar Republic* (Oxford: Routledge, 2014).

Goldhagen, *Daniel Jonah, Hitler's Willing Executioners: Ordinary Germans and the Holocaust* (London: Abacus, 2007).

Hoffmann, Peter, 'The German Resistance and the Holocaust', in *Confront! Resistance in Nazi Germany*, ed. John Michalczyk (New York: Peter Lang, 2004).

Spielvogel, Jackson J, '*Hitler and Nazi Germany: A History*', (Oxford: Routledge, 2016).

Wheatcroft, Andrew & Overy, Richard, *The Road to War: The Origins of World War II* (London: Vintage, 2012).

Kolb, Eberhard, *The Weimar Republic* (Oxford: Routledge, 2008).

Schumann, Dirk, *Political Violence in the Weimar Republic, 1918-1933*, trans. Thomas Dunlap (Oxford: Berghahn Books, 2012).

Contents

Foreword	vii

Sample Paper One
Section A: Source Analysis	3
Section B: Sources/Interpretations	11

Sample Paper Two
Section A: Source Analysis	25
Section B: Sources/Interpretations	31

Sample Paper Three
Section A: Source Analysis	41
Section B: Sources/Interpretations	45

Sample Paper Four
Section A: Source Analysis	55
Section B: Sources/Interpretations	59

Foreword

If you're enrolled on Edexcel's History GCSE, you will required to complete a paper known as a "modern depth study." Schools have a choice of different time periods and topics to cover for the modern depth study, and this book (as you might have guessed from its title!) is designed to guide students through the module on Weimar and Nazi Germany, 1918-1939.

Now, before anything else, it's important to briefly outline what this paper looks like. The paper is comprised of two sections. The first section is the shorter of the two. At the start of this section, you will be presented with a single primary source (usually an image, but occasionally a text-based source) and you will then face two questions. The first question (worth 4 marks) will ask you to make inferences from the source, while the second (worth 12 marks) will require you to write what we might describe as a mini-essay (in total, then, this section is worth 16 marks).

Once you've cleared that hurdle, you'll have the second, longer section to contend with. You will be presented with 4 sources: two will be primary sources (they can be either images or text), and two will be secondary sources, which are usually brief snippets of writing from professional historians (the exam board calls these "Interpretations"). You will then have to tackle Question 3 – though this is a bit misleading, because Question 3 is in fact broken into four separate parts.

Question 3(a) is worth 8 marks, and requires you to compare the usefulness of the two new primary sources. Question 3(b) and 3(c) are both worth 4 marks each (so 8 in all) – the first will ask you to identify the difference between the two historians' interpretations, while the second will ask you to explain *why* these historians differ. Finally, you have 3(d), which is a 20 mark essay question that requires you to engage with both the interpretations while also using your own knowledge.

I fully appreciate that this may all sound complex and daunting, but don't despair – as you work through this guide, the very talented Loughlin (the author!) will take you through things step-by-step and shine a light into the paper's every nook and cranny.

And yet, having said all that, it is important to emphasise that this guide is *not* merely designed to familiarise you with the paper's structure. Rather, this guide – by proffering model answers, dissecting this exemplar material, and painstakingly delving into Edexcel's mark-schemes – will seek to demonstrate *how* to ensure you are covering all bases and picking up every available mark. For while it is true that the sources and many of the questions are unseen and thus you can never prepare fully in advance, there are all sorts of tactics and techniques that you can memorise and master before you set foot in that exam hall. In fact, it's precisely because we felt that no other guide adequately grapples with these techniques – adequately spells out how best to approach the paper's assorted challenges – that we decided to put together this dedicated technique guide for this exam in the first place!

In short, our hope is that this book, by demonstrating *how* to tackle the paper's challenges, will help you feel more confident in doing so yourself. I believe that it is also worth mentioning that for many of the questions you'll encounter in this paper – and this especially applies to the longer, essay-style questions – there is no one answer the examiner is looking for. That is, while Loughlin's work may represent "model" material, someone else's answers could be quite different and yet be just as effective at nabbing the marks. I won't pretend your exam is likely to be *fun* – my memory of the exams is pretty much the exact opposite. But still, this is one of the very few chances that you will get at GCSE level to actually be a little bit creative. And to my mind at least, that was always more enjoyable – if *enjoyable* is the right word – than simply demonstrating that I had memorised loads of facts.

R. P. Davis, 2021

Sample Paper One

Section A: Source Analysis

Study Source A below and then answer Question 1.

Source A: Political posters during the 1932 presidential election. On the right, it reads 'Vote on 13 March for Adolf Hitler', 'The Reichspresident is Adolf Hitler', and, loosely translated, 'Enough is enough!' On the left, the poster of Hindenburg entreats the electorate to 'Vote for a person, not a party'.

Question 1: Guidance

Question 1 assesses source evaluation (AO3). First off, let's actually take a look at how Edexcel defines AO3 in more detail: it requires us to 'analyse, evaluate and use sources' in order to make 'substantiated judgements, in the context of historical events studied'.

The question itself, which is worth four marks, is broken into four parts. You are required to make two inferences from the source – and for each inference, you need to offer details from the source that supports your inference.

So *what is an inference*? An inference is a conclusion you can draw from a source – something that you are able to deduce from inspecting or reading the source. So imagine you were presented with a photo of your school: the school is empty, and there's a woman with a large OFSTED badge outside putting up a sign that reads: 'Closed: Not Fit For Purpose'. What can you infer?

Well, you can infer that the school has been closed down by OFSTED.

That would be your inference.

But you then need to support your answer with details from the source: this is what Edexcel mean by 'substantiated judgements' – a judgment that is rooted in substance.

You would point to the words on the sign – they explicitly tell you that the school has been closed. You would also point to the OFSTED badge the woman is wearing, which implicitly suggests that OFSTED are behind the closure. You would then mention that OFSTED is a governmental organisation that, in twenty-first century Britain, regulates schools.

That very last bit – about OFSTED being a governmental organisation – is fulfilling that final element of AO3, which wants you to put details you can see in the source 'in the context of historical events studied'. OFSTED is an important organisation due to the wider historical context of it being empowered by the British government.

Right, so back to your exam.

You will be presented with a source, usually (but not always) an image, which portrays some significant aspect of life in interwar Germany. To answer the question, you will need to make two conclusions (or inferences), and you will then need to explain both inferences by drawing on details from the source *and* by tying these details into your knowledge of the historical period.

Section A: Source Analysis

I find it is often useful, first and foremost, to take stock of the date of the source and think back to the key events in that time period. This source, for example, falls into the period of the Great Depression and the Nazis' rise to power, 1929-1933.

Question 1: Exemplar

Give two things that you can infer from Source A about the Nazis' rise to power.

[4 points]

(i) What I can infer:

The Nazis claimed to offer strong leadership to combat Germany's economic and political issues.

Details in the source that tell me this:

The iconography of the strong Aryan worker in the Nazi poster, breaking out of chains, resonates strongly with the Nazis' rhetoric, that the country was being held back from greatness by politicians, socialists, and Jews. The caption 'Schluss jetzt!' implies that, once the Nazis come to power, the strikes, unrest, and economic hardship will come to an end.

(ii) What I can infer:

Hitler's opponents were counting on the reputation of Hindenburg to keep the Nazis at bay.

Details in the source that tell me this:

Hindenburg was supported as President by a coalition of different political factions, including establishment conservatives and social democrats. The caption 'vote for a person, not for a party', suggests that they were counting on Hindenburg's reputation as a safe pair of hands. By generalising the Nazis as an undifferentiated 'party', they may also have hoped to downplay Hitler's charisma and his party's broad appeal.

Question 2: Guidance

Question 2 is a meatier question – it's worth 12 marks in all – and these are split between AO1 and AO2, which are both worth 6 marks apiece. Of course, this begs the question: what are AO1 and AO2?

Edexcel defines AO1 as the ability to 'demonstrate knowledge and understanding of the key features and characteristics of the periods studied.' The key words here are **knowledge** and **understanding**. **Knowledge** is all about demonstrating that you have information up your sleeve about the time period under discussion, whereas **understanding** is about your comprehension of these events – in other words, knowledge would be showing you know an attempted coup took place on a specific date, whereas understanding would be indicating (either explicitly or implicitly) that you understand that a coup is an attempt to illegally overthrow a government. A good way of demonstrating **understanding** is simply to make clear that you have selected a certain set of facts and figures based on their relevance to the question.

Next up, we have AO2, which Edexcel say is about the ability to 'explain and analyse historical events and periods studied' – and to do so using 'second-order historical concepts'.

Let's first linger on the words 'explain' and 'analyse'. **Explaining** is all about deploying the knowledge you've invoked to explicitly answer the question and to make an argument. If the question was asking you to explain reasons why a country's government collapsed, your explanation might involve a discussion about how the failed coup you've brought up contributed to the government's collapse a few years later.

Analysis is about taking a step back, looking at various factors, and weighing their merits. Was the failed coup the only factor, or are there other factor that are more important? In short, to demonstrate **analysis** you must show you understand that no historical argument is completely flawless, and illustrate your awareness of potential counter-arguments and alternative explanations.

You will notice that Question 2 always asks you, implicitly or explicitly, to debate differing explanations for a historical trend or event. In other words, the necessity to engage in analysis is built into the very phrasing of the question.

What about that strange phrase 'second-order historical concepts' that also appears in AO2? The mark scheme says that these are ideas relating to 'causation, consequence, similarity, difference, change, continuity and significance.' In my view, if you are going about explanation and analysis the right way, you will be considering ideas relating to cause and consequence as you go along, as well as engaging in comparisons that will ensure you touch on 'similarity', 'difference' and 'significance'.

Combined, then, AO1 and AO2 involve **knowledge** and **understanding**, **explanation** and **analysis**. This means you will have to demonstrate that you know the important events of the period (**knowledge**), **understand** how they fit together, can **explain** why they are important, and can **analyse** their significance relative to each other.

As an aside, you might be interested to know that this combination of AO1 and AO2 is inspired by a well-known educational concept called Bloom's Taxonomy, where basic learning skills build up to advanced skills. For more insights into the way that **knowledge**, **understanding**, **explanation** and **analysis** interrelate, you may want to look up Bloom's Taxonomy and investigate further!

Finally, the fact this is a twelve mark question can also help guide us with the length and structure of our answer. We want to make at least three fully-developed points to pick up all the marks; so let's give each of these points their own paragraphs, and sandwich them between an introduction and a conclusion.

Question 2: Exemplar

Explain why the Nazis were able to consolidate their power in Germany in the years 1933-39. You may use the following in your answer:

- police state
- employment policies

You **must** also use information of your own.

[12 points]

1) *I begin by flagging up that I'm aware of the time period under discussion, and why this time period was chosen.* **2)** *A useful way of answering this type of question is to think of the economic, political, and social aspects of the question. Also, by bringing up various competing factors, I'm alerting the examiner that I'm aware of AO2's demand that I engage in comparative analysis.* **3)** *Refer to the prompts (those bullet points beneath the question!) early and explicitly in your answer, to ensure the examiner picks up on them. Also, note how I link the Great Depression causally to the economic hardships — I'm hitting a 'second order concept' of causation that'll earn me AO2 marks.* **4)** *Knowledge: specific historical facts. Also, I'm implicitly demonstrating my understanding that the knowledge I'm invoking relates to the Nazis' employment policies. I'm hitting AO1 for both knowledge and understanding.* **5)** *By tying these measures to the Nazis' broader objectives, I'm continuing to demonstrate the relevance of the knowledge to the question, scoring me further AO1 for understanding.* **6)** *Explanation: here I am now explicitly using the knowledge I've invoked to answer the question — I'm explaining how the Nazis used employment policies to consolidate power, thereby hitting AO2.* **7)** *Not only am I furthering my explanation, but the phrase 'more segments' is hinting that there is more to the story (there are other segments to consider!), and thus gesturing towards upcoming analysis.* **8)** *I'm relating back to the phrasing of the question, to tell the examiner that I'm still on topic.* **9)** *I'm stacking up knowledge, thus scoring AO1. Moreover, the very fact I am bringing in a second point means I'm implicitly engaging in analysis (AO2), because I'm weighing up different factors.*

Following Hitler's appointment as Chancellor in 1933[1], it might have seemed as though the Nazis' control of Germany was total — but there were still significant challenges standing in the way of their consolidation of power. These included economic issues, opposition from political opponents, and opposition from society more broadly[2].

The catastrophe of the Great Depression continued to cause significant economic hardships after 1933, which were addressed by Nazi employment policies.[3] Hitler used his position as Chancellor to grant concessions to unemployed workers — including giving Nazi Party members a guaranteed job — while at the same time curtailing the rights of trade unions, and eventually abolishing them.[4] Agricultural labourers, who had suffered terribly during the Great Depression, were given bread and celebrated as the lifeblood of the nation.[4] This placed these destitute groups at the centre of the Nazis' nationalist story.[5] The unemployed had mainly supported the Communists in the 1920s, so these policies managed to marginalise the Nazis' political opponents, while at the same time tying Hitler's chancellorship to mass employment and national revival.[6] Hitler's economic policies therefore legitimised his leadership by bringing more segments of German society on side.[7]

Although the Nazis were the largest party in the Reichstag after the 1932 election, they did not hold a majority of seats, and so Hitler's chancellorship was vulnerable to political opposition. An opportunity to consolidate power[8] came with the Reichstag fire,[9] which Hitler blamed on the Communists.[10] This gave the Nazis the leeway to suspend civil liberties with the Enabling Act of 1933, and the death of Hindenburg the following year allowed Hitler to declare himself President as well as Chancellor.[11] By 1934 these changes had allowed Hitler to complete his consolidation of political power.[12]

Having consolidated control over the economic and political levers of power in Germany[13], the Nazis were then free to victimise their social critics, who were no longer protected by freedom of speech or political opposition, by creating a police state. Hitler eliminated internal threats from the SA in 1934 during the Night of the Long Knives, established the Gestapo as a secret police force, and ensured the loyalty of the German military by decreeing that they take the Hitler Oath.[14] Military officers and other aristocratic conservatives' approval was won with Hitler's expansion of the military, in violation of the hated Treaty of Versailles.[15]

By 1935 all of Germany's leaders had either been won over to the Nazis, or were languishing in concentration camps, and no meaningful political or social opposition remained.[16] *However, the Nazi consolidation of power was not total: underground resistance continued throughout the 1930s and beyond among youth groups like the swing kids and the White Rose, while some military officers like Stauffenberg were plotting Hitler's assassination.*[17]

10) I am not only bringing in knowledge, but demonstrating my understanding of its relevance. 11) Explanation (AO2). This goes a step further than understanding – I'm now explicitly answering the question: how does this relate to the Nazis' consolidation efforts? 12) Analysis: I'm indicating that the Nazis' methods I've just discussed were very effective in consolidating political power – a judgement that takes us into the realm of analysis. Note also that I have given an awareness of chronology (thus gesturing to second-order concepts of causality, AO2), while once again relating back to the phrasing of the question. 13) Here I am 'signposting' my points, to show that I am developing an argument. Moreover, I'm engaging in analysis – I'm indicating that the Nazis' efforts to victimise critics as a means of consolidating power was facilitated by the previous factors already mentioned. In a sense, I am comparing the significance of the factors I'm discussing – a hallmark of both analysis, and a nod to the word 'significance' mentioned in 'second-order historical concepts'. So: AO2 marks aplenty! 14) Knowledge (AO1) – this is the springboard for any given point. 15) I am indicating my understanding of the relevance of the information I've been discussing, hence AO1. Moreover, I'm starting to gesture towards an explanation of how all this victimisation aided the Nazis in their consolidation of power. 16) I hammer home the explanation of my third point at the start of the conclusion... 17) ...and then pivot to analysis. I'm indicating here that I'm aware of potential counter-arguments, which is the sort of weighing up and judgement-making that defines analysis.

Section B: Sources/Interpretations

Question 3: Overview

Question 3 has four parts, based on two sources and two interpretations, and in order to answer successfully you will have to demonstrate that you can think like a historian. You will be given four items to consider: two pieces of primary evidence (which can be images or text), and two interpretations drawn from secondary sources, usually history books.

It is important here to keep the point distribution in mind – the four parts to question 3 are worth 8, 4, 4, and 20 marks respectively (so that's 36 marks in all). You should use this as a guide to how much time to spend on each question, and how many points to hit in each section.

Again, the idea here is to build up your analysis over the span of all four questions. Begin by evaluating the sources (the phrasing of question 3(a) is 'how useful is...'), then compare and contrast the differing interpretations of the historians in 3(b).

In 3(c), use your insights from (a) and (b) to connect the information in the sources to the historians' interpretations, and explain how they might have used evidence to reach their conclusions.

Finally, in question 3(d) draw everything together, add some insights of your own from your knowledge of the period, and analyse the pros and cons of the historical argument.

In many senses, Question 3 is not one question; it's four questions. But don't feel daunted. We shall tackle them one by one!

Section B: Sources/Interpretations

Question 3: Sources and Interpretations

Source B: Prince Bernhard von Bülow, *Revolution in Berlin*.

In this extract, Prince von Bülow, a former Chancellor of Germany from 1900-1909, gives his impressions of the chaotic birth of the Weimar Republic in 1919.

Our new masters were unfit to govern. Most characteristic of their mentality was the speech from the Reichstag steps, delivered by Scheidemann, an ex-imperial state secretary, who, in proclaiming the republic, began his oration with the following: 'The German people have won all along the line.' A stupid lie! And a very cruel piece of self-deception! No, alas, the German people had not 'won' – it had been conquered, overpowered by a host of enemies, wretchedly misled politically, reduced by famine, and stabbed in the back!

To any unbiased spectator of these events, to whoever watched it all in the one hope that the German nation might not perish, these first days of our republic were days of the return to chaos. Children could scarcely have done worse.

Source C: Election poster for the Centrist Party, 1930, depicting fascists and communists fighting beneath a bridge labelled 'Centre'.

Interpretation 1: from *The Third Reich in Power* by Richard J Evans, published in 2006.

Many people have tried to explain how [the Nazis] managed to achieve such a position of total dominance in German politics and society with such speed. One tradition of explanation points to long-term weaknesses in the German national character that made it hostile to democracy, inclined to follow ruthless leaders and susceptible to the appeal of militarists and demagogues. But one can see very little evidence of such traits. Liberal and democratic movements were no weaker than they were in many other countries... [Hitler] possessed one great gift: the ability to move crowds with his rhetoric. His party, founded in 1919, was more dynamic, more ruthless and more violent... They modified their specific policies according to their audience, playing down their antisemitism where it met with no response.

Interpretation 2: from *The Weimar Republic* by Ruth Henig, published in 2014.

The reality was that Germany in the 1920s was politically, socially and economically a very unstable and divided society, and this led political parties to appeal ever more intransigently to their own particular section of the electorate... Parties found it difficult enough to adjust to a democratic political framework, after the highly autocratic rule of Wilhelmine Germany... the demobilisation of the army left hundreds of thousands of young men disorientated and thirsting for some sort of action. They found it fighting on the streets against political opponents... With public confidence so lacking in the new democratic republic, the task of stabilising the economy was an impossible one.

Question 3(a): Guidance

Question 3(a), like Question 1, revolves around AO3 – the assessment objective that gauges our ability to 'analyse, evaluate and use sources', and it's worth a total of 8 marks.

The question always takes the same format. It will get you to look in detail at Sources B and C, and it will ask you how helpful they are for explaining some event or trend that took place during the period of study.

In the mark scheme, we are told that, in the very best answers, 'judgments on source utility for the specified enquiry are given, applying valid criteria'. This is a roundabout way of saying that you need to conclude how useful each source is, and you need to have strong, convincing reasons to back up your decisions. We are also told that, when justifying their verdict, top-level students must also be taking into account a source's 'provenance' – in other words, the source's origin (where it came from and who it is by) – so this is also something crucial you need to be covering.

Finally, the mark scheme says that to score the highest marks, 'contextual knowledge' must be used 'in the process of interpreting the sources and applying criteria for judgments on their utility.' In plain English: you need to bring in your own knowledge of the time period when assessing the utility of each source.

So to summarise: you need to **tell the examiner how useful each source is** and **offer good reasons** to back your arguments up. And you need to bring in **the sources' provenances** and **your own knowledge** as you go about arguing your case.

A simple (but effective) way of structuring this answer is to dedicate a paragraph to each source. I'd also propose adding an extremely brief introduction – we're talking a single sentence – in which you answer the question directly (I'll show you what I mean below). I'd also suggest adding a slightly longer conclusion, in which you take a step back and offer a parting thought for the examiner to ponder on.

Question 3(a): Exemplar

3(a): Study Sources B and C.

How useful are Sources B and C for explaining the challenges facing the Weimar Republic in the years 1919-1933?

Explain your answer, using Sources B and C and your own knowledge of the historical context.

[8 points]

Sources B and C highlight two different vulnerabilities facing the Weimar Republic, so each is useful in giving a partial picture of events.[1]

Source B gives the viewpoint of the aristocratic military establishment, which viewed the new republic with scepticism from the very start.[2] This is illustrated by the phrase 'stabbed in the back' – a reference to the rumour that the German army in the First World War had been betrayed by cowardly politicians in 1918.[3] This faction was primarily fearful of communism, and supported Hindenburg's coalition with the Nazi Party in 1933, which provided an air of legitimacy to Hitler's government. In this sense, this tendency was fundamentally anti-democratic, and represented a persistent challenge to the Weimar Republic.[4]

Source C illustrates the deep divisions in German society, and the highly fragmented and polarised state of electoral politics throughout the Weimar period. The image of fascist and communist groups fighting in the streets was not an allegory, but a reality: from the Spartacist uprising of 1919 to the Kapp Putsch of the Freikorps and the Beer Hall Putsch of the Nazi Party, popular politics in the Weimar period played out in the streets[5] While the Catholic Centre party (the religious support for which is indicated by the cross)[6] attempted to rise above this violence, this lofty stance rendered them a political irrelevance.

What is not illustrated in these sources,[7] however, is the existence of issues which unified large sections of the German public – unemployment, economic chaos and currency devaluation, a long-standing antisemitism, and a lingering popular resentment over the humiliations of the Versailles Treaty.

1) First, answer the question directly. I am explicitly telling the examiner that both have a degree of utility in assessing the challenges facing the Weimar Republic. **2)** I'm immediately flagging up my awareness of Source B's provenance – namely, the fact we are hearing from an individual drawn from the military establishment. **3)** Note here how I quote directly from the source – a superb way to demonstrate that I'm properly engaging with it – then add my own knowledge of context. Remember: the examiner is expecting a display of contextual knowledge from top-level candidates. **4)** At the end, I relate it back to the question by explaining the 'challenge facing the Weimar republic' indicated by the source. I am, in short, gesturing towards the source's utility. **5)** Here again, the source is tied to wider contextual knowledge. In this way, I address AO3, the objective for this question, by giving a 'substantiated judgment' of the interpretation. **6)** Another bit of contextual information here. **7)** No source will give the whole story – so it's important also to note what the sources don't tell us. Indeed, this is just as important as acknowledging the ways in which the sources are useful. Moreover, the content here also shows an awareness of context, which – as explained earlier – is another key thing to demonstrate to maximise marks.

Section B: Sources/Interpretations

Question 3(b): Guidance

Although 3(b) is a smaller question – it's worth four marks – we are for the first time in this paper encountering AO4, which is described by Edexcel as the ability to 'analyse, evaluate and make substantiated judgements about interpretations (including how and why interpretations may differ) in the context of historical events studied.'

Briefly, in plain English, this means that we are going to have to make judgements about historians' interpretations of events, while deploying our awareness of context.

Now, question 3(b) – like 3(a) – will always take the same basic format. You will be asked to look closely at the two interpretations provided, which will both be talking about the same topic – perhaps a particular event, perhaps a historical trend – and to identify the main difference between these two interpretations, using details from both.

Before we dive in, however, it's good to look at what the mark scheme tells the examiners to look for in the very top scoring answers. *I know, I know* – focusing on the mark scheme can sometimes suck the excitement out of history. But if we want to score all the points, we need to know where the goalposts stand.

In top-scoring answers, we are told, 'the interpretations are analysed and a key difference of view is identified and supported from them'. So we need to be identifying a key difference between the interpretations, using information from the interpretations to demonstrate to the examiner what you mean. But also, remember to be exhibiting your awareness of historical context, as that's another component of AO4.

Interestingly, the mark scheme does not tell the examiner to expect students to identify one difference in particular; rather, it indicates that any sensible difference that is backed up by evidence will be credited.

Below, I'll show you how I advise to tackle this question – that is, by tackling one interpretation at a time.

Question 3(b): Exemplar

3(b): Study Interpretations 1 and 2. They give different views on the vulnerabilities of the Weimar Republic in the years 1919-1933.

What is the main difference between the views?

Explain your answer using details from both interpretations.

[4 points]

Interpretation 1 argues that there was nothing inevitable about the Nazis' rise to power, that German democratic traditions were as strong as any other country's and could have resisted them.[1] Evans suggests that the personal charisma of Hitler, the ruthlessness of his party, and the way he tailored his political messaging allowed the Nazis to take advantage of a turbulent situation.[2]

Interpretation 2 suggests that German democracy was systemically vulnerable, and predisposed to dictatorship.[3] Henig points out that the autocratic legacy of Kaiser Wilhelm, and the highly militarised nature of German society, hamstrung the ability of a democratic government to act and set the stage for the Nazis' rise to power.[4]

1) This one is pretty straightforward. The main difference... 2)...Supported by specific details from the interpretation. 3) And once again. The main difference... 4)...Supported by specific details. Remember, we are addressing AO4: first evaluate the sources, and second, place them in context.

Question 3(c): Guidance

3(c) is another shorter, four-mark question and also revolves around AO4. Moreover, it again always takes the same format: you must give one reason *why* the two interpretations differ.

In a sense, then, 3 (c) is a kind of continuation from 3 (b): we are taking that difference you identified in 3(b) and trying to understand why it has arisen.

Here's how the mark scheme describes a top-scoring answer: 'An explanation of a reason for difference is given, analysing the interpretations. The explanation is substantiated effectively.' In plain English, we need to give a reason why the two historians see things differently, while again rooting that explanation in information drawn from the interpretations.

I'd suggest that you start off by giving the reason for the difference from the outset – this need not be more than a sentence long, and it should get right to the heart of the matter. I'd then suggest you elaborate by tackling each interpretation in turn.

Let's take a look at an exemplar...

Section B: Sources/Interpretations

Question 3(c): Exemplar

3(c) Suggest one reason why Interpretations 1 and 2 give different views about the vulnerability of the Weimar Republic in the years 1919-1933.

You may use Sources B and C to help explain your answer.

[4 points]

One reason might be that the two interpretations highlight different historical aspects of the German political system. Evans emphasises Germany's long liberal tradition, and the continuing activities of the Centre Party in 1930 (Source C) suggest that this remained important in the Weimar era. Henig, by contrast, emphasises the continuing influence of German militarism, which is embodied in the sceptical reaction of von Bülow to democratic government in Source B.

Question 3(d): Guidance

The most heavily weighted question in the paper, Question 3(d) is worth 20 points, and 16 of these marks are reserved for AO4 (the other four are for spelling, punctuation and grammar). It is, in short, a type of essay question.

The question will ask you how far you agree with one of the two interpretations you've been given. However, the question is more nuanced, because it makes it clear that, in the process of explaining the degree to which you agree with the interpretation, you also need to bring in the *other* interpretation, as well as your own knowledge in the form of historical context.

As ever, let's look at how the mark scheme describes a top-level answer.

First, such an answer, we are told, ought to provide 'an explained evaluation reviewing the alternative views in coming to a substantiated judgement' and 'precise analysis of the interpretations' while 'indicating how the differences of view are conveyed and deploying this material to support the evaluation'.

So, in plain English, a strong answer will demonstrate familiarity with the competing views one might have on the event or historical trend under discussion – this includes the two views of the historians you've been given, but also potentially other views you've been made aware of in your studies.

Moreover, a strong answer will also make reasoned judgements on the merits of these various views, making use of elements of the two historians' interpretations

– be it the information the historians make use of, or how they make their argument – as a means of backing up the argument.

Next, the mark scheme tells us that the strongest answers include 'relevant contextual knowledge' that has been 'precisely selected to support the evaluation'.

In other words, when evaluating the pros and cons of different historical views, it is not enough to simply refer to the interpretations; you also need to be bringing in your own contextual knowledge.

Finally, the mark scheme says that the best answers make an 'overall judgment' that has been 'justified' and have a 'line of reasoning [that] is coherent, sustained and logically structured'.

Really, it's saying two things here. First, that you will need to make an overall judgement on the degree to which you agree with the interpretation mentioned in the question. And second, while the mark scheme does not say how you must structure your essay, it must be done in a way that is rational, convincing and articulate – and keeps up all of these attributes throughout.

It feels like a lot of moving parts, right? But let's take a deep breath and think about how we can structure this in a way that ensures we are ticking all these boxes. Here's my suggestion:

- **In the short, opening paragraph**, hone in on the interpretation the question explicitly invites you to comment on, and very quickly outline what you see as the strengths and weaknesses of the argument.

- **In the second, longer paragraph**, elaborate on the aspects of the interpretation you find most convincing. At this point, bring in your own knowledge in order to back up your reasoning.

- **In the third paragraph**, bring in the other source, and discuss how it shows a different point of view – potentially one that the first source neglects. In the process, make sure it is clear to the examiner that the first source, then, is not seeing every angle. Also, keep on injecting your own knowledge

- **In the fourth paragraph**, bring in other angles or point of views that both sources neglect to touch on.

- **In the fifth paragraph**, give your opinion on both of the interpretations – which one do you agree with more? And, of course, how far do you agree with the interpretation explicitly mentioned in the question?

Question 3(d): Exemplar

3(d): How far do you agree with Interpretation 2 about the vulnerabilities of the Weimar Government? Explain your answer, using both interpretations and your knowledge of historical context

[20 points]

Interpretation 2 presents a strong case for the political weakness of the Weimar government, but ignores some of the Weimar government's successes in restoring Germany's economy and culture.[1]

Henig argues that there were three interrelated vulnerabilities of the Weimar Republic: the lack of a strong political tradition, which reduced politics to a brawl between interest groups; large numbers of ex-soldiers engaged in street violence; and a deep public distrust of democratic government.[2] She highlights the strong influence of German militarism, and the continuation of pre-First World War attitudes, as a major contributing factor. Indeed, the attitudes of pre-War politicians like von Bülow were mirrored in the political position of establishment politicians like Hindenburg in the 1920s.[3] These attitudes were clearly popular among the large population of ex-soldiers, 9 million of whom returned to a broken country after World War I. This is indicated by the Kapp Putsch of 1920, as well as the widespread resentment of the Treaty of Versailles, and it was clearly seized upon by the Nazis, whose popularity was bolstered by their use of militaristic imagery and calls for national strength.

However, this interpretation does not provide the whole story.[4] As Evans points out,[5] there was a long liberal tradition in Germany. Indeed, a wide spectrum of democratic parties attracted mainstream support, notably the Catholic Centre Party and the Social Democrats. The Weimar government, with Stresemann as foreign minister, began to recover from 1924: the Rentenmark provided monetary stability, and the Dawes Plan rearranged Germany's reparation payments. This indicates that the Weimar government was able to function to some extent.[6]

Additionally, neither interpretation notes the unparalleled cultural and scientific advances that took place in Weimar Germany, which was at the forefront of physics, architecture, film, art, and literature in the 1920s.[7] Moreover, the early coalition-building efforts of the Social Democrats, bringing military elites and trade unionists together to form a government, indicates that these groups were perhaps not always so deeply divided as Henig suggests.[8]

1) First, answer the question directly. 2) Here, I indicate that I know what the interpretation is arguing. Note that I haven't simply regurgitated the information from the passage, but categorised it into a broader argument. 3) I present supporting evidence from Source B, as well as my own knowledge, to explain how Henig might have come to this conclusion. 4) Now that we've presented the evidence for Henig's view, we look at some counter-arguments. 5) Interpretation 1. 6) And now, some evidence which presents a different argument to Henig's. Note that at the end of the paragraph, I refer back to the essay question, indicating that the Weimar government may not have been that vulnerable in the mid-1920s. 7) Now, we move beyond the sources and interpretations given to us, and begin to expand our argument using additional knowledge of the period. Note also the use of guiding words throughout (however, additionally, moreover) to increase readability. 8) Refer back to the question once again.

Overall, I am more convinced by Evans' contention: namely, that the Nazis' rise to power was not an inevitable consequence of the vulnerabilities of the Weimar government.[9] The continuing influence of German militarism was clearly important, and a deep anti-democratic streak is discernible in the attitudes of both elites and ordinary people during the Weimar period. However, the recovery of the mid-1920s, the broad coalition of political interests in the same period, the vibrancy of Weimar Germany's culture, and the manipulative tactics which had to be employed by the Nazis to gain power, all suggest that the political vulnerabilities of Weimar Germany were not as significant as Henig contends.

9) *And now, to conclude. We come to an explicit judgment, and back it up by restating our arguments.*

Sample Paper Two

Section A: Source Analysis

Study Source A below and then answer Question 1.

Source A: March, 1933: Otto Wels, a Social-Democratic representative in the Reichstag, speaks out against the Enabling Act.

Since there has been a German Reichstag, never before has the control of public affairs by the people's elected representatives been reduced to such an extent as is happening now – and will happen even more, through the new Enabling Act. The expansive power of the government must also have serious repercussions, as the press too lacks any freedom of expression.

The gentlemen of the National Socialist Party call the movement they have unleashed a national revolution... the destruction of that which exists does not make a revolution. The people are expecting positive accomplishments. They are waiting for effective measures against the terrible economic misery that exists not only in Germany but in the whole world.

Question 1: Guidance

Sometimes, the inference question will ask you to analyse a written text, rather than an image. However, the process is the same – to make an inference (which, as explained earlier, is sort of like an educated guess or deduction), and then to support this inference using the contents of the source.

It's important to note that you're unlikely to get full marks for this question if you simply list your observations; the examiner will be looking for evidence that you've thought *beyond* the information that's presented in the source. In other words, you will need to provide an assessment of what the source says *explicitly* (i.e. the actual wording of the source), and *implicitly* (i.e. what the source implies/hints at, or tells us about the wider history).

My advice? Begin by looking for details within the source, and then think about what wider trends or events might be inferred from them. In this example, we are given a speech from a Social-Democrat politician. Explicitly, he criticises Hitler's government for abolishing civil liberties and neglecting the welfare of the German people. What might he be saying implicitly?

In your answer, it's best to quote directly from the source if possible, but you can also paraphrase or flag up key words, as in the example below.

Question 1: Exemplar

1. Give **two** things that you can infer from Source A about the Nazis' rise to power. (4 points)

(i) What I can infer

The source suggests that the Enabling Act, among other policies, stripped power from the Reichstag representatives, and placed it in the hands of the Nazis.

Details in the source that tell me this

Wels says that the "control of public affairs" has been "reduced" to an unprecedented degree, and will be further reduced by the Enabling Act.

(ii) What I can infer

The Enabling Act led to the destruction of representative democracy in Germany.

Details in the source that tell me this

I know this because the source not only notes the "serious repercussions" unleashed by the Act, and its "destruction" of representative democracy, but also claims these are not "effective measures against the terrible economic misery" facing Germans.

Question 2: Guidance

As already mentioned, the exam questions for this paper follow a fairly regular formula.

When it comes to Question 2, it will always be on a topic drawn from one of four time periods: the early instability of Weimar, 1918-1923; the period of recovery, 1924-29; the rise of the Nazis, 1929-32; and building a dictatorship, 1933-39. This periodisation might also be reflected in your school textbook. Question 2 in particular seems to focus on one of these four periods in detail. Note that any of these periods can come up, and you are sure to be asked about more than one – so don't focus your revision too narrowly.

On the day of the exam, you are likely to be nervous about forgetting salient facts and figures. After reading through the whole exam paper, it can be a good idea to jot down a few notes, headings, and prompts which you can then return to as you draft your answers. For example, you might read this question and immediately think of Germany's monetary problems and international treaties. Note down 'Locarno Treaty – Kellogg-Briand Pact – Dawes Plan – Stresemann – Rentenmark – Reichsmark – Young Plan', perhaps with dates if you remember them (although examiners will be looking for comprehension, rather than chronology, so don't worry if you can't remember specific dates). When it comes to drafting your answer, you can then concentrate on answering the question instead of worrying about whether or not you'll forget a key piece of information.

When it comes to planning this question, I have already noted in the 'Guidance' to Question 2 in Paper One that I suggest an introduction, a conclusion, and three content paragraphs. Think of these internal paragraphs as 'themes' – in each paragraph, you tackle a different theme or factor.

You are given two bullet points beneath the question, and you can use these as the basis for two of your three 'themes' – though you can also pick your own themes, if you so wish. As was noted in the 2018 Examiner's Report, the 'stimulus points' – which what they call those bullet points – are 'useful reminders', but 'candidates do not need to use these stimulus points'. The important thing, according to the Examiner's Report, is that students exhibit 'depth of knowledge, shown by three discrete aspects of the question being covered.'

In other words, make sure you're covering three 'themes'!

Finally, the 2018 Examiner's Report also notes that the 'question does not require a judgement to be made' or 'for the answer to prioritise…factors'. So you do not need to be giving a final verdict on which factor you personally believe to be the most important.

Question 2: Exemplar

Explain why the Weimar government's policies were able to stabilise Germany in the period 1924-1929.

You may use the following in your answer:

- Dawes Plan
- Social reforms

You **must** also use information of your own.

[12 points]

Between 1924 and 1929, the Weimar Republic entered a period of stability, following successive social and economic upheavals in the aftermath of the Armistice. There were three main reasons for this:[1] the stabilisation of the German economy with Stresemann's negotiations, the normalisation of international relations, and the institution of new social reforms which brought civil rights, job opportunities, and cultural growth.

With the French occupation of the industrial Ruhr valley, and the punitive repayments imposed by the Treaty of Versailles, Germany's economy was in ruins, with hyperinflation reducing the value of the German Mark to practically zero.[2] Without a functioning currency, Germany could not meet its payment obligations, and the economy ground to a halt.[3] In 1923, the Chancellor Gustav Stresseman introduced a new currency, the Rentenmark, putting up Germany's land and industrial property as backing. The plan succeeded, and the following year Rentenmarks were replaced by a new gold-backed currency, the Reichsmark.[4] The recovery was

1) In the first paragraph, the question is directly addressed and the three topics to be discussed are clearly stated. 2) I'm displaying my knowledge – a key aspect of AO1 – while also hinting at my understanding that the knowledge I'm injecting relates to economic concerns.
3) Here my understanding is increasingly apparent: not only do I know about the hyperinflation, but I also understand its implications.

further strengthened by a renegotiation of the Versailles payment terms under the Dawes Plan, and again under the Young Plan. This economic recovery allowed a solid grounding for social stability over the next five years.[5]

Other outstanding issues relating to the Treaty of Versailles were also resolved in the 1920s, reintegrating Germany into the international community and further stabilising the country.[6] In 1925, the Locarno Treaty fixed Germany's borders and led to the French withdrawal from the Ruhr. The 1928 Kellogg-Briand Pact further attempted to ensure peace in Europe by outlawing the waging of wars of aggression. Locarno allowed Germany to regain its position as a fully sovereign European state, and to join the League of Nations. As a result, German pride was partially restored, and the influence of fascists and militarists over the public was somewhat attenuated.[7]

The stability of the mid-1920s was not confined to economics and politics alone, however. Large-scale social reforms were also enacted, including legal protections for civil rights, the freedom to join trade unions, and regulations on working hours and health insurance. These reforms reduced unemployment among ex-soldiers and increased production, further stabilising the economy. As a result,[8] both the left-wing and right-wing opponents of the government lost support.

Therefore, Stresemann's negotiations and other government reforms stabilised Germany by strengthening the economy, renegotiating some of the harsher terms of the Treaty of Versailles, and enacting social reforms.[9] While these measures did provide stability, the shock of the 1929 crash[10] would plunge Germany back into economic catastrophe, and undo much of Stresemann's work.

4) I am bringing in still more knowledge – namely, the economic measures Stresemann took to deal with the issues I've covered – as well as introducing it in a way that signals my understanding. However, I am also now starting to hit the explanation criteria of AO2: I'm starting to explicitly answer how the Weimar government attempted to stabilise Germany via economic means. Moreover, by flagging cause and effect – namely, that Stresseman's measures succeeded – I'm again hitting AO2 marks: I'm acknowledging 'second-order' historical concepts. **5)** *I'm now hitting the Analysis criteria of AO2: I'm taking a step back, and assessing the degree to which the economic measures stabilised Germany's economy.* **6)** *Reiterating the question, to illustrate that we're still on track.* **7)** *Note that at the end of every paragraph, there is a 'so what' sentence – it answers the question that the examiner will be asking at this point: 'So what? How did all of these things you mention contribute to the stability of Weimar Germany?'* **8)** *Use phrases that emphasise your awareness of cause and effect. As the mark scheme says, a key AO2 target here is 'analysis of second order concepts: causation'.* **9)** *Just a quick summary of the preceding paragraphs as I broach the conclusion.* **10)** *The 1929 crash brings us right up to the end of the period under discussion, and allows us to mention another key event. I'm showing off knowledge and understanding, while also taking a 'step back' and giving the sort of alternative perspective that will score us AO2 Analysis marks.*

Section B: Sources/Interpretations

Source B: Victor Klemperer, a Jewish professor who lived in Germany throughout the Nazi period, writes about the boycotting of Jewish businesses, 31 March 1933.

The boycott begins tomorrow. Yellow placards, men on guard. Pressure to pay Christian employees two months salary and to dismiss Jewish ones. No reply to the impressive letter of the Jews to the President [Hindenburg] and to the government... No-one dares make a move... In Munich, Jewish university teachers have already been prevented from setting foot in the university.

Source C: Newspaper photograph taken in Berlin during the anti-Jewish boycotts, 1933. The placard reads, 'Germans! Defend yourselves! Do not buy from Jews!'

. . .

Interpretation 1: Daniel Jonah Goldhagen, *Hitler's Willing Executioners: Ordinary Germans and the Holocaust*, published in 2007

Because the party leaders knew that antisemitism permeated their constituencies, including the working class, at the end of Weimar the political parties did not attack Hitler's antisemitism, although they attacked him on many other grounds... for antisemitism hundreds of thousands were ready to ascend the barricades, to fight brawls in public halls, to demonstrate in the streets; against antisemitism hardly a hand stirred.

Interpretation 2: Peter Hoffmann, 'The German Resistance and the Holocaust', in John Michalczyk, ed., *Confront! Resistance in Nazi Germany*, published in 2004

There was a German resistance movement... church-oriented groups as well as Jehovah's Witnesses insisted on the preservation of their forms of worship; there were Jewish underground groups; there were non-conformist youth groups; there was the White Rose Munich student group who secretly distributed leaflets protesting against the mass murder of the Jews... and there were Communist groups. All of these groups were quite unequipped to bring about Hitler's downfall from within.

Question 3(a): Guidance

To refresh your memory, the question asks about the 'utility' of the source material — in other words, what can (and can't) this source tell us about a historical question? For full marks you must give a judgment on the source's utility, how it relates **to the question being asked**, and whether or not its usefulness is affected by its 'provenance', or its origin — all the while adding contextual knowledge into the calculation.

Remember: examiners will specifically look for discussion of the source's provenance. Have you considered where the source originated, and whether it contains a particular perspective or bias? Assessing sources, and coming to a judgment on how trustworthy or representative they are, is another of the key skills of the historian.

Also, when tackling 3(a), be careful not to spend time commenting on which source is more useful, as there are no marks in play for that here. As the 2018 Examiner's Report notes: 'a few candidates took the unnecessary additional step of trying to determine which source was 'most useful' which is not the focus of the question and therefore is not rewardable.' Examiner's Reports can be a really useful place to work out what *not* to do.

Question 3(a): Exemplar

3(a): Study Sources B and C.

How useful are Sources B and C for understanding the Nazis' anti-Jewish policies?

Explain your answer, using Sources B and C and your own knowledge of the historical context.

[8 points]

Source B is useful for understanding the Nazis' anti-Jewish policies because it gives a first-hand account from one of their victims. Klemperer recounts a feeling of being totally abandoned by the government and his fellow citizens, none of whom are willing to "make a move", or to speak out against injustice.[1] It also illustrates some of the Nazis' specific policies, such as dismissing Jewish workers and academics, and enacting wage discrimination. Its provenance, as the immediate thoughts of a victim of discrimination living through this event, gives us powerful emotional and experiential information as well.[2] One limitation[3] to its usefulness is its date of creation, at the very beginning of Hitler's chancellorship – thus it cannot tell us how these policies evolved over time.

Source C is useful because it shows the boycott in effect. It portrays the use of signs and slogans to mark out the Jewish population, and the role of the SA in enforcing the boycott with brute force. The necessity of having SA men enforcing the boycott illustrates both the Nazis' dominance of street-level politics, and also suggests that not all resistance to the Nazis had diminished by 1933. Its provenance, a newspaper photograph, also gives an indication of the view the rest of the world had of Germany at the time.

1) I quote directly from the source, to illustrate that I am using specific information from the source to assess its usefulness. **2)** *When discussing provenance, think about the relationship between the creator of the source and the events it is describing. What insight can we gain from this source which might be missing from, for example, an official report or a newspaper article?* **3)** *No source is comprehensive; all have some limitations, such as a limited perspective, partial knowledge of a situation, or bias.*

Question 3(b): Guidance

For questions 3(b) (and indeed (c)), you are invited to contrast two different interpretations of a historical event. It's important to note here that, among historians, differences in interpretation tend to be differences of degree – usually, historians will be working from the same collection of sources and evidence, so it would be quite unusual if they had a completely different understanding of the facts! Instead, differences will arise from historians placing different emphases on the sources they've examined, or interpreting the significance of sources differently. They may also be trying to answer two different questions: for example, the question 'was there resistance to the Nazi regime?' is different to the question 'how widespread was the resistance to the Nazi regime?'

Question 3(b): Exemplar

3(b): Study Interpretations 1 and 2. They give different views on the extent of Germans' resistance to the Nazis' antisemitic policies.

What is the main difference between the views?

Explain your answer using details from both interpretations.

[4 points]

Interpretation 1 argues that antisemitism was endemic within German society, and was not primarily stoked by the Nazis. It suggests that the other political parties in Weimar Germany did not explicitly attack the Nazis' antisemitism, instead focusing on other aspects of their programme. It further contends that the mass politics of the late Weimar era illustrates the extent to which antisemitism was deeply-rooted in Germany.

Interpretation 2, by contrast, highlights some of the strands of opposition to antisemitism, linking it to the opposition to Hitler's regime explicitly. It suggests that there were significant pockets of dissent in German society – from communists to students to Jehovah's Witnesses – who agitated against Nazism and against antisemitism. However, the source also implies that these groups were small, isolated, and largely independent of one another, and so could not mount an effective opposition.

Question 3(c): Guidance

Candidates sometimes try to argue that the interpretations differ as a result of their publication history and provenance – that is, as a result of its date or place of publication – but this is *not* something you want to be discussing when you tackle 3(c). As the 2018 Examiner's Report puts it, 'it is not possible to provide effectively substantiated reasons why the interpretations are different based on such things as where and when the interpretations were published.' In other words, if one interpretation was published online, and the other in a book, this is *not* something you should be commenting on.

Once again, Examiner's Reports are an invaluable source of information on what to avoid!

Question 3(c): Exemplar

3(c): Suggest one reason why Interpretations 1 and 2 give different views on the opposition to antisemitism.

You may use Sources B and C to help explain your answer.

[4 points]

One reason why the two interpretations may differ is that they are concerned with slightly different questions.[1] Whereas Interpretation 2 focuses on the small pockets of resistance to Nazism, Interpretation 1 is instead concerned with the attitude of the German public as a whole. Klemperer's writing in Source B seems to illustrate the low visibility of effective resistance movements against antisemitism – he notes that a letter of protest to the government has received no reply. Both sources also show the widespread appeal of antisemitism across the German population, from the university professors of Munich to the working class ex-soldiers of the SA.[2]

1) Interpretations may also give different weights to causal factors, or examine a question with a different area of focus. 2) Note here that, like in Question 1, I am both describing the source and also inferring information from it.

Question 3(d): Guidance

In the guidance to the previous paper, I put forward a structure for how one might tackle the extended answer for question 3(d). However, it is important to keep in mind that there is flexibility when it comes to structure.

Whereas in my previous model answer I had five paragraphs, in this one I have four; however, the overall structure is still pretty similar. I'll outline the structure I've employed now, and you can compare it with the structure I employed in the previous paper

- A short introduction that answers the question: I answer outright the degree to which I agree with Interpretation 1.

- A longer second paragraph that delves into the aspects of Interpretation 1 that I find convincing, while using my own knowledge to back up my reasoning and rationale.

- A meaty third paragraph in which I bring in Interpretation 2, and discuss how it brings in another point of view that implicitly draws attention to what Interpretation 1 overlooks. This is combined with my own knowledge that draws attention to other points of view still.

- A concluding paragraph that renders verdicts: how far do I agree with Interpretation 1? Do I find it more or less convincing than Interpretation 2? Why?

Remember: **paying attention to both interpretations is non-negotiable**. As was noted in the 2018 Examiner's Report: 'There is no expectation that both interpretations are dealt with in equal depth but both should be examined explicitly.'

Question 3(d): Exemplar

3(d): How far do you agree with Interpretation 1 about Germans' opposition to antisemitism? Explain your answer, using both interpretations and your knowledge of historical context.

[20 points]

1) First, answer the question. 2) Summarise the argument made in Interpretation 1. 3) Reference the sources for supporting evidence: a good way to show off your ability to cross-reference different types of evidence. 4) Supplement your answer with your own knowledge of relevant facts. This is used to help show what I consider the strengths of Interpretation 1.

Interpretation 1 presents a convincing argument[1] that antisemitism "permeated" German society even before the Nazis came to power, and notes that very few voices were raised against anti-Jewish hatred in the Weimar era.

Goldhagen claims that political parties were reticent to defend German Jews as this was unpopular with the electorate, and that tens of thousands of Germans rioted and demonstrated in support of antisemitic causes.[2] This is reflected in Source B, which portrays Victor Klemperer's feeling of vulnerability and isolation – he writes that "No-one dares make a move" against the Nazis.[3] Source C, showing the antisemitic boycott of 1933, also reveals the extent of antisemitic feeling in Germany, only a few days after Hitler became chancellor. This suggests that antisemitism had already been a feature of German politics for some time. Indeed, much of the opposition to the Versailles Treaty of 1918 was animated by the 'Dolchstosslegende', the conspiracy theory that the German army had been 'stabbed in the back' by Jews, leading to the German defeat.[4] The communist uprisings, strikes, and trade union agitation of 1918-19 were also blamed on Jews, and some German churchmen preached antisemitic sermons long before the Nazis began to influence the churches in the 1930s.

Interpretation 2, by contrast, highlights the resistance movements to Nazism, particularly the White Rose students and their vocal opposition to the Nazis' antisemitic policies. Other groups, like the Edelweiss Pirates, opposed the Nazi regime in general, rather than antisemitism in particular.[5] In any case, support for these groups was limited to a small minority, whereas millions of Germans – over ten percent of the population – were members of the Nazi Party, and millions more actively or passively supported the regime.[6] Political indoctrination of children, via the Hitler Youth, and social control through media, religion, and the secret police, meant that few resisted the pressure to conform to Nazi doctrine. Hoffmann recognises the inability of these groups to effect change in Germany, writing that "all of these groups were quite unequipped to bring about Hitler's downfall."

5) *Discuss the counter-argument (or in this case, difference in emphasis) of Interpretation 2.* **6)** *Further use of supplementary knowledge. I use this to probe Interpretation 2 and to show my nuanced approach to Hoffmann's point of view, implicitly laying bare its strengths and weaknesses.* **7)** *Reiterate your answer to the question, and add your own thoughts and analysis. Remember: you need to be hammering home your final verdict at this point.*

Ultimately, I think that Interpretation 1 makes the stronger, and more important, point.[7] Viewing the horrors of Nazi Germany in hindsight, it is comforting to think of them as an aberration: a moment of collective madness in a country held to ransom by fascist thugs. We like to think that we would have been on the 'right side of history'. Goldhagen reminds us that these horrors had deep roots in society and culture and that ordinary Germans, simply living their lives, also had a share of culpability. This is a lesson of vital importance for our own times.

Sample Paper Three

Section A: Source Analysis

Study Source A below and then answer Question 1.

Source A: Poster produced by the Freikorps militia in 1920, with the caption 'Who will save the Fatherland? German men! Soldiers of all weapons! Join our ranks!' It evokes the nationalist image of the Lützow Corps of volunteers who fought against Napoleon in 1813.

Question 1: Guidance

Students often find interpreting images to be more difficult than interpreting text. Therefore, this guide will give two more examples of image interpretation. Remember that you need to both make observations about the source itself, and then place these observations within your wider knowledge of the period.

Question 1: Exemplar

Give **two** things that you can infer from Source A about the instability in Weimar Germany between 1918 and 1924.

[4 points]

(i) What I can infer

The Freikorps targeted disaffected ex-soldiers.

Details in the source that tell me this

The source calls on "soldiers of all weapons" to join the Freikorps, uses martial imagery, and evokes the historical Lützow volunteer fighters.

(ii) What I can infer

There was a widespread feeling of social decline in Germany in the early 1920s.

Details in the source that tell me this

The phrasing of the poster, asking 'Who will save the Fatherland?' indicates that the audience felt Germany was in peril, and traditional German ways of life were under attack. The historical imagery of the poster, harkening back to idealised nationalist heroes, serves to reinforce the difference between the glorious past, and a degraded present.

Section A: Source Analysis

Question 2: Guidance

While the criteria for this question only requires you to make three points, explain them, and give factual evidence to support them, it can aid the structure of your answer, and indeed highlight the salient points for the examiner, to add short introductory and concluding sentences. These mini introductions and conclusions should clearly lay out your three main points and reiterate how they address the question.

This mode of structuring an answer (or any piece of persuasive writing) is sometimes called the 'say it three times' model – i.e. tell the reader how you're answering the question, answer it, and reiterate the answer you've just given. This means that, if your answer becomes wordy or unfocused, the examiner is less likely to miss your point and mark you down.

Question 2: Exemplar

Explain why the Nazis' policies aimed at women in the years 1933-39 had such a significant impact.

You may use the following in your answer:

- Employment policies
- Control of religion

You **must** also use information of your own.

[12 points]

During the Weimar years, a climate of social liberalism had afforded women new rights and expanded horizons in society. The Nazis were determined to return women to their 'traditional' roles, in the following ways: through a reform of employment policy, through the influence of German churches and civil society, and through specific policies relating to marriage and the family. [1]

Under the Nazis, the Law for the Reduction of Unemployment incentivised women to stay out of the labour force, in order to ensure the availability of jobs for male party members. In practice, this had the effect of removing women from secure, well-paid employment, and pushed many into more precarious jobs instead. In the

1) I'm flagging to the examiner in the introduction what my three 'themes' are going to be. Really try to hold your examiner's hand – make it as easy as possible for them to digest how you are tackling things.

1930s, the numbers of women in employment actually rose by 2.4 million, but their job security was markedly decreased.[2]

The Nazis believed that women's lives should revolve around the 'Three Ks' — Kinder, Kirche, Küche, or children, church, and kitchen. Following Hitler's concordat with the Catholic Church, and his attempts to control the contents of sermons in Protestant churches, this message was also reinforced from the pulpit.[3] *Dissenting priests, like Martin Neimöller, were sent to concentration camps. However, in the face of widespread opposition from priests, the Nazis eventually had to curtail this policy of social control.*[4]

In addition to taking control of women's economic and spiritual lives,[5] *the Nazis also enacted a number of specific policies to keep women in the home, raising children. From a young age the League of German Maidens instructed girls to aspire to a life of domestic child-rearing. There were monetary incentives for marriage and childbirth, and women who had large families were given medals and state honours. The improvements to the economy probably had a large effect on increasing the birth rate as well.*[6]

In this way, the Nazis sought to undo many of the changes that modernity had brought to women's lives in the 1920s.[7] *Through the social policies of the 1930s, the Nazis imposed their vision of traditional family values, and ensured an increased level of control over women's financial, spiritual, and personal lives.*

2) It's not necessary to quote dates and statistics chapter and verse, but if you're able to retain them, it may help your mark. After all, knowledge is a key component of AO1. 3) Here, contextual information about related Nazi policies is used to develop a point. Note, however, that I begin and end the paragraph with direct references to the question. 4) If the material that comes earlier in the paragraph explains the effect of the Nazis' policies on women, this extra detail gets us thinking about the extent *of these effects, which takes us into the realm of analysis. Remember: AO2 requires us to both explain and analyse. 5) Signposting. We are ensuring that the examiner is kept abreast of our arguments. 6) Notice how I use the language of cause and effect. I am scoring marks for discussing those "second-order concepts" that also contribute to AO2.*
7) I'm relating back to the first sentence, and giving a sense of chronology.

Section B: Sources/Interpretations

Source B: Hermann Führbach, a factory worker from Mulheim-Glatz, writes in 1934 about why he joined the Nazi Party:

The end of the war and the revolution [of 1919] are events which I can still remember vividly. What I felt to be a particular disgrace was an incident in which Red revolutionaries stopped some officers and, right in front of our eyes in the schoolyard, ripped off their epaulettes.*

... It was in 1923 that I first heard about the Hitler movement. I quit the [trade] union and joined the defence league called German Eagle... When the French marched in [to the Ruhr], I got a lot of work from the German Eagle... From that point on, I fought untiringly against communists, Marxists. On July 4th 1926, I took the oath on the flag before the Führer... I knew that Germany had a leader again.

Epaulette: a decorative shoulder strap on a uniform, sometimes containing an indication of rank.

Source C: Photograph of a Nuremberg Rally, 1937. These massive propaganda spectacles attracted thousands of spectators and participants.

WEIMAR AND NAZI GERMANY, 1918-1939

Interpretation 1: Jackson J. Spielvogel, *Hitler and Nazi Germany: A History*, published in 2016

Supported by their slogan of the national revolution, the Nazis entered the [1933] election campaign. They were well financed as a result of large contributions now coming in from industrialists. In their appeals to the industrial magnates for financial support, Hitler and Göring emphasized that this would be the last election in Germany... the Nazis made effective use of the power of the state. State-directed public radio, a new and powerful political instrument, was monopolized by the Nazis. Hitler's speeches were transmitted throughout the country... Millions of new voters had been attracted to Hitler and the prospect of a new Germany.

Interpretation 2: Andrew Wheatcroft and Richard Overy, *The Road to War: The Origins of World War II*, published in 2012

The conservatives gave Hitler a foot in the door; they did not expect him to beat it down and ransack the house. But the movement was almost uncontrollable. In 1933, the young men of the Party, brought up on street violence, suddenly found the law on their side. They took revenge on all the enemies of the 'new Germany': on trade union officials and communists; on moderate socialists and Catholics; on artists and writers of the avant-garde; and on the Jews. By the end of the summer Germany was a one-party state, the trade unions were destroyed, democratic government replaced by the authority of the *Führer*.

Question 3(a): Guidance

In the 2019 Examiner's Report, we learn that 'The best responses were those that were able to address "how useful" by establishing the strengths sources have as

Section B: Sources/Interpretations

evidence before determining how far the limitations affect their usefulness.' In other words, when you bring up a source, make sure you lead with its strengths before you move onto its drawbacks.

Also, while it is important to look at provenance and how it impacts reliability, this must not be the only thing you discuss when assessing utility. This, according to the 2019 Examiner's Report, is a trap many students fall into. It notes that although 'it is important for candidates to remember that judging utility may involve some comments about reliability', those 'answers which focus solely on this criterion do not fully consider the value of the sources as evidence'.

Question 3(a): Exemplar

3(a): Study Sources B and C.

How useful are Sources B and C for understanding the popularity of the Nazi Party? Explain your answer, using Sources B and C and your own knowledge of the historical context.

[8 points]

Source B is the firsthand account of a Nazi Party member. It is useful in explaining how ordinary Germans were radicalised in the 1920s, and what caused them to join the Nazis.[1] In Führbach's case, the disrespect shown by communists towards army officers, and his Nazi affiliation ensuring him stable employment, were his main reasons for joining. This parallels the attitudes of many Germans at the time, who felt that Germany, and the German army in particular, had been humiliated, that Germany's leadership was weak, and that the country was in danger from communists.[2] As it is written by a Nazi supporter in 1934, shortly after Hitler came to power, we cannot expect this source to give an unbiased view of the Nazis, or mention any of their negative aspects.[3]

Source C portrays the Nuremberg rallies, large public spectacles designed to give the impression of a united German people, singularly devoted to the person of the Führer. The photograph gives an indication of the scale of these events, and the powerful iconography and staging that brought home this message.[4] The dais lit up against the darkness, looming over thousands of flag-toting devotees, gives the impression of Hitler as being in total control of the state. It is, obviously, a propaganda image, and therefore while it can tell us about the symbolic power of Nazi iconography, and the seri-

1) Usefulness of the source; i.e. what can this type of source material tell us, that other sources might not? 2) Supplementing my interpretation with my own knowledge of the historical context. 3) Discussion of the source's bias. Notice that this comes after I've established the aspects of it I deem to be useful. 4) Usually, image sources are examined for the historical information they contain, but in the case of propaganda images, you may also want to discuss their artistic composition, and the feelings they are intended to evoke.

ousness with which the Nazis took their imagery, it tells us very little about the realities of life under the Nazi regime.

Question 3(b): Guidance

A key thing to remember about 3(b) is that you are not just pointing out that, say, Interpretation 1 talks about fact X and Interpretation 2 talks about fact Y. Rather, you are digging down into their *views*: that is, their opinions, their points of view, and their emphases on things.

I know what you're thinking: *I bet we're going to get yet another quote from an Examiner's Report…* And you're precisely right, because, to my mind, Examiner's Reports are as crucial as the mark scheme when it comes to understanding what is expected from us. And to quote from the 2019 Examiner's Report: 'It is important for candidates to remember that the focus of this question is to identify the differences between the views rather than identifying differences of surface detail'.

Question 3(b): Exemplar

3(b): Study Interpretations 1 and 2. They give different views on the Nazis' consolidation of power.

What is the main difference between the views?

Explain your answer using details from both interpretations.

[4 points]

While Interpretation 1 focuses on the Nazis' use of the levers of power, Interpretation 2, by contrast, emphasizes[1] the speed with which the institutions of the state were torn down by the Nazis.

Interpretation 1 emphasizes the support from German elites that allowed Hitler to come to power. It notes that German industrialists handsomely financed the Nazis in the 1933 election, because they were weary of the years of political instability that had come before. Indeed, Hitler had only become Chancellor with the connivance of Prussian Junker elites in the conservative party. The source also highlights the importance of new technology – the Nazis used

1) As aforementioned, the differences between many historians' interpretations is really a difference in emphasis.

the radio to spread their message of "national revolution" all across Germany, and used their control of state apparatuses, including the Interior Ministry, to silence their opponents.

Interpretation 2, by contrast, focuses more on the Nazis' broad appeal, and on the violent methods by which they secured victory in the election. It emphasizes the mass outbreak of street violence which now had "the law on [its] side", with Göring as interior minister. Rather than highlighting the rise in support for Hitler that Interpretation 1 emphasizes, Interpretation 2 focuses on the elimination of the Nazis' enemies.

Question 3(c): Guidance

Differences of views can arise between historians for all sorts of reasons. Is one historian perhaps asking a different question than another? Is one placing emphasis on a different segment of society than the other? Is one thinking, for instance, about the economy, while the other is thinking more about political factors? Or perhaps they are relying on different kinds of sources (remember, you are allowed to invoke sources B and C – and these can sometimes be a clue)? These are the sorts of questions you need to be asking yourself!

Question 3(c): Exemplar

3(c): Suggest one reason why Interpretations 1 and 2 give different views on Hitler's consolidation of power. You may use Sources B and C to help explain your answer.

[4 points]

One reason is that the two interpretations are focusing on different sections of society. Interpretation 1 places a greater emphasis on politics at the elite level, while Interpretation 2 focuses more on the impact of street-level politics.[1] These views are not necessarily incompatible, however.[2] Source C illustrates the Nazis' masterful use of the power of the state for propaganda purposes, but without the mass mobilisation of the SS and other Nazi organisations, the Nuremberg Rallies could not have been held. Source B emphasizes the importance of anti-communism and the role played by Nazi party members in dominating German society, but without the support of big industrialists and landowners the

1) Political history often focuses on different classes or social groups in its analysis. This can be a good way of thinking about differences in interpretation. 2) The two Interpretations you are given may not be diametrically opposed; you are allowed to note this.

Nazis may not have been able to guarantee Führbach (Source B) a job, and he and many like him may not have been swayed to Nazism.

Question 3(d): Guidance

As well as the main assessment criteria for Question 3(d) – AO4 – there are also four points up for grabs for 'spelling, grammar, punctuation, and use of specialist terminology'. It is therefore important to leave enough time in the exam to read through your answers and check for clarity, spelling, and sentence structure. Moreover, it can be useful to brush up on some historical terms of art – such as 'primary source' or 'historiography' – as well as subject-specific terminology like 'Sonderweg', 'Dolchstoss', and 'Junker'.

In many of your history papers, but this one especially, you may be asked to write about historical events which continue to evoke strong feelings today – from the Holocaust, to the Atlantic slave trade, to the wars, famines, and revolutions that permeate human history. It is important to learn about this history precisely because it still animates a strong response in the present, and you are encouraged to explore the parallels with contemporary issues of prejudice and racism, exclusionary nationalism, war, terror, and injustice.

A word of warning, however: historians are not politicians. Their primary purpose is to examine historical events and to draw conclusions based on evidence, not to make political speeches about current events. However much an examiner might be moved by your impassioned call to action, they will only be able to award points for your examination of the sources and interpretations provided, and your knowledge of historical events. So, make sure that your enthusiasm for the subject doesn't impede your ability to answer the question in a meticulous and disciplined manner. You don't need to provide a blandly 'neutral' viewpoint (indeed, in Question 3(d) you are required to take a side!), but you should attempt, as much as possible, to provide an objective and evidenced one.

Question 3(d): Exemplar

3(d): How far do you agree with Interpretation 2 about the Nazis' consolidation of power? Explain your answer, using both interpretations and your knowledge of historical context

[20 points]

I find Interpretation 2 to be a broadly convincing argument for the Nazis' consolidation of power. It makes references to three major aspects of the Nazis' rise: their political manoeuvring, their manipulation of the public's fears and resentments, and Hitler's personal charisma.

In the 1933 election, despite the Nazis already beginning to consolidate[1] their hold on the levers of power, they failed to secure an outright majority of votes, winning over only 44% of the electorate. Hitler negotiated a coalition agreement with the conservatives, which, in the words of Wheatcroft and Overy, gave him "a foot in the door", becoming Chancellor and expanding his influence among conservative reactionaries. He placed allies in positions of power over the police and army, allowing his stormtroopers to intimidate political opponents with impunity. These political manoeuvres allowed Hitler to pass the Enabling Act, suspending civil liberties, outlawing opposition parties, and imposing a dictatorship, after the Reichstag burned down later that year.

1) *As far as possible, use the phrasing of the question. This will ensure that your answer doesn't lose focus.* **2)** *Here, I go beyond the information in the Interpretation and add my own contextual knowledge to advance my argument.* **3)** *While it is not the most artful stylistic choice, repeatedly returning to the question prompt is a good way to reassure the examiner that you are addressing the question.* **4)** *And now, I examine the perspective of Interpretation 1, and explain why it is less convincing.*

Wheatcroft and Overy also emphasize the overarching importance of the Nazis' success in tapping into fears and resentments within German society. Both Interpretation 2 and Source B emphasize the fear of communism as a central reason for the growth in support for Nazism, and also a factor in the growth of Nazi Party membership. Furthermore,[2] the speed with which the Nazis moved against their many enemies in 1933-4 – including incarcerating trade unionists, Catholics, cultural elites, and Jews in concentration camps – illustrates that the Nazis faced little resistance from civil society. Thus, the Nazis' ability to create a climate of fear in Germany, and to enforce it with the SA, was also key to their consolidation of power.

Finally, Wheatcroft and Overy note that by 1934 "the authority of the Führer" was absolute. This alludes to Hitler's personal charisma as a leader, something which can also be seen in Sources B and C, in the large crowds attending the Nuremberg Rally and in Herman Führbach's phrase "I knew that Germany had a leader again". Without this cult of personality, Hitler could not have commanded the loyalty of the SS, SD, the Gestapo, and the army, who formed the blunt end of the Nazis' consolidation of power.[3]

Interpretation 1, on the other hand,[4] while it makes important points about Hitler's political acumen, his increasing support from business and landed elites, and his use of new technologies to spread his message, it under-emphasises the significance of Nazism as a mass movement, and the legacies of the street violence from which it was born. For this reason, I find Interpretation 2 to be a more convincing account of the important factors leading to Hitler's rise.

Sample Paper Four

Section A: Source Analysis

Source A: Hitler announces the Anschluss with Austria at the Reichstag, 1938

Question One: Exemplar

Give **two** things that you can infer from Source A about Hitler's dictatorship.

[4 points]

(i) What I can infer

Hitler was successful in crushing his political opposition.

Details in the source that tell me this

All of the Reichstag delegates seem to be unanimously supporting the Anschluss – there is no sign of political opposition in this highly choreographed propaganda image.

(ii) What I can infer

Nazi Germany was a highly militarised society.

Details in the source that tell me this

A large number of the senior officials surrounding Hitler are wearing military uniforms, as is Hitler himself.

Question Two: Exemplar

Explain why there was a rise in support for the Nazi Party in the years 1929-1932.

You may use the following in your answer:

- Great Depression
- Political failure

You **must** also use information of your own.

[12 points]

Three main causes of the rise in support for the Nazis were: many Germans' mistrust of democratic government and its increasing inability to govern in the early 1930s; the effects of the economic collapse and the Great Depression; and fear of a communist takeover of Germany.

Despite the successes of the Weimar Republic in stabilising the country in the mid-1920s, many Germans remained sceptical of democratic government, including the long-serving president, Hindenburg, and his supporters in the aristocratic Prussian Junker class and the army. This mistrust was shared by large sections of the electorate, who were frustrated by the still-ongoing reparation payments to the Entente Powers, and by policies of the Weimar government which were seen as keeping Germany weak. This was reflected in a growing Nazi Party membership, which reached 130,000 by 1929. In the period 1929-33, the Nazis successfully converted this increased support into an ever-increasing number of seats in the Reichstag.

The electorate's mistrust of the government was deepened with the economic collapse of 1929, caused by the calling in of American loans. The economic mismanagement and political deadlock which characterised the Müller and Brüning governments further angered the electorate, leading to rising support for the Nazis and the Communists. The rapid rise in unemployment, which peaked at over 30% in 1932, further fed the rise in support for extreme parties, who offered decisive (and often violent) solutions, new job opportunities, and convenient scapegoats for the nation's ills. The Nazis proposed a "national revolution", in which the cure for society's ills was to be found in "traditional" German societal values.

The Nazis were able to make more significant gains than the Communists in the Depression years by playing on a fear of communism. While the Communists garnered large support from urban industrial workers, the Nazis were able to tap into a broad constituency, including conservative farmers and small business owners, nationalists and militarists, and landowners and business elites, all of whom were fearful of appropriations under a Communist government. The Nazis deliberately positioned themselves as bringers of national unity, with their slogans of "national revolution" and "Volksgemeinshaft", or people's community.

Thus, by 1932 the Nazis were able to play on widespread fears of communism, distrust of democratic institutions, and the failure of the Weimar Republic to deal with the Great Depression, to attract thousands of new party members and win a plurality* of seats in the Reichstag the following year.

*Plurality: the largest number of votes, but not a majority.

Section B: Sources/Interpretations

Source B: Manifesto of the Spartacists, 1918

The revolution has made its entry into Germany. The masses of soldiers, who for four years were driven to the slaughterhouse for the sake of capitalistic profits, and the masses of workers, who for four years were exploited, crushed, and starved, have revolted. That fearful tool of oppression - Prussian militarism, that scourge of humanity - lies broken on the ground.... Proletarians of all countries... We ask you to elect workers' and soldiers' councils everywhere that will seize political power and, together with us, will restore peace.

Source C: Troops in Berlin during the Kapp Putsch, March 1920.

Interpretation 1: Eberhard Kolb, *The Weimar Republic*, published in 2008

The threat from the left provoked a strong defensive reaction, not only from the middle class but from supporters of social democracy... it was only in co-operation with the corps of officers and the traditional bureaucracy that they could maintain order and solve day-to-day problems... [the Social Democrats] rejected the Spartacist tactics of using street demonstrations and rallies to whip up the emotions of the anonymous masses whose political stability could not be taken for granted.

Interpretation 2: Dirk Schumann, *Political Violence in the Weimar Republic, 1918-1933*, published in 2012

There is no doubt that the events of March 1920 added new dimensions to the experiences with violence from the previous year. This was the first time the counterrevolutionary forces had tried to change the state of affairs by force... Among the bourgeois public, the [Kapp Putsch] was sharply and unequivocally condemned, though understanding was also voiced for the sympathizers among the population. The putschists themselves were clearly dissociated from the right and denounced... The sort of highly emotional charges that were usually levelled against the radical left were thus redefined and now aimed at the radical right.

3(a): Study Sources B and C.

How useful are Sources B and C for understanding the threats to the Weimar government in the years 1919-1923?

Explain your answer, using Sources B and C and your own knowledge of the historical context.

[8 points]

Sources B and C illustrate the two threats to the Weimar Republic from the political extremes, Source B from the left and Source C from the right.

Source B is a publication of the Spartacist movement outlining their beliefs. It shows the major areas from which the communists drew their support – industrial workers and disaffected members of the German armed forces. Indeed, one of the first triggers of the German Revolution was the revolt of Kriegsmarine sailors in Wilhelmshaven and Kiel. It also gives an indication of some of the dangers posed by the Spartacists to traditional German society: it attacks the idea of Prussian militarism, which was highly prized by officers and landowners, and it calls for a worldwide revolution, and the overthrow of governments. The source gives us important information on the aims of the Spartacists, but cannot tell us how those aims translated into reality.

Section B: Sources/Interpretations

Source C portrays the Freikorps taking control of Berlin during the Kapp Putsch, and therefore reveals another major threat to the stability of the Weimar Republic. The government had employed the Freikorps, militia units made up of World War I veterans, to crush the workers' militias in 1919, but the following year they attempted a coup d'etat led by Kapp. This photograph illustrates the Freikorps' access to military hardware and transportation, and the presence in the foreground of what look like officers illustrates the support the Freikorps had from the conservative officer class. While the image captures something of the chaos of Berlin in 1920, it presents only a partial view, and does not give us much information on the wider course of events.

3(b): Study Interpretations 1 and 2. They give different views on the threats to the stability of the Weimar Republic.

What is the main difference between the views?

Explain your answer using details from both interpretations.

[4 points]

The two interpretations emphasize different threats to the stability of Weimar. Interpretation 1 highlights the "threat from the left" as an early danger to the Weimar government, which whipped up a populace "whose political stability could not be taken for granted." It also notes that, in response to this threat, the Weimar government came to rely on reactionaries within the officer corps.

Interpretation 2 argues that the Kapp Putsch brought "new dimensions" of challenge to the Weimar Republic. The danger to the government is clearly stated, as the Freikorps "tried to change the state of affairs by force." The source further notes that the middle class rejected this early attempt at military rule.

(c) Suggest one reason why Interpretations 1 and 2 give different views on the threats to the Weimar Republic. You may use Sources B and C to help explain your answer.

[4 points]

The interpretations differ in that they highlight two different threats to the existence of the Weimar Republic. While each gives weight to different causes for Weimar's collapse, this does not necessarily mean that the sources cannot agree: it could be that the threat of communist revolution in 1919, and of a military coup in 1920, were equally serious and presented existential threats to the Weimar Republic. Interpretation 1 is given support from Source B, which alludes to the Spartacist's aims of international revolution, and their intention to seize political power. Interpretation 2 is given support from Source C, which portrays heavily armed soldiers occupying the streets of Berlin.

(d) How far do you agree with Interpretation 2 about the threats to the Weimar Republic in the years 1919-1923? Explain your answer, using both interpretations and your knowledge of historical context.

[20 points]

I agree with Interpretation 2's assessment of the rightwing threat to the Weimar Republic as being more significant than the leftwing threat. It presented a more prescient threat because of the widespread militarist and anti-democratic sentiment existing within German society, because of the extent to which the Weimar government had to rely on army officers and aristocratic landowners in order to govern, and because of the limited and fragmentary support for the communists.

Both interpretations make reference to the reactions of the middle classes, and it therefore seems apparent that both historians regard the middle class as the political linchpin of German politics in this period. Despite the fact that the reaction to both the Spartacist revolt and the Kapp Putsch from the middle class was intensely negative, the inherent traditionalism and militarism of the middle class nonetheless preserved their approval for right-wing factions, from whom "the putschists themselves were clearly dissociated" (Interpretation 2). This continued support for the extreme right is illustrated by the broad base from which the Nazis would draw their support: farmers, small shopkeepers, professionals, and social elites. Despite the military's attempt to take power in 1920, the German public still largely approved of the army, and its aristocratic political leadership.

This presented a further threat to the Weimar government, precisely because the Social Democrats had to rely on the army leadership to "maintain order and solve day-to-day problems" (Interpretation 1). This reliance did not come to an end with the crushing of the revolutionary workers in 1919, but was a recurring feature of the Weimar Republic right up until 1933, with the government relying more and more on the unifying figure of President Hindenburg in order to pass any legislation. Moreover, much of German civil society was sympathetic: when rightwing gangs began assassinating government functionaries, including the foreign minster Walter Rathenau, in 1922, they were often released or only given light sentences. Likewise, after the Beer Hall Putsch in 1924, Hitler was only incarcerated for nine months. The right wing threat was thus more significant because it was a constant menace from within the government itself.

Finally, although there was widespread leftwing resistance from soldiers' and workers' councils in 1919, these originated from a number of fragmentary groups and failed to produce a coherent programme or greatly affect the representation of the government. The Spartacists had strong support in Berlin, but this support did not extend across the country. A revolutionary government was set up in Bavaria, and a 'red army' of workers fought with the Freikorps in various cities, but outside of industrial areas the movement attracted little support, and "provoked a strong defensive reaction, not only from the middle class but from supporters of social democracy". (Interpretation 1). Therefore, although the uprisings of 1919 presented a serious challenge to the Weimar Republic, they did not present as large or pernicious a threat as the anti-democratic right.

Thus, because of the continuing public approval of "Prussian militarism" (Interpretation 1) among the German people, because of the support for rightwing anti-democratic movements by elements of the Weimar government and civil service, and because of the fragmented and weak support for the Communists, I agree with Interpretation 2's characterisation of rightwing groups as a more prescient threat to the Weimar Republic.